MW00831412

Keeping Advent
and Christmastime

LITURGY
TRAINING
PUBLICATIONS

Acknowledgments

The translation of the psalms, the Canticles of Zechariah, Mary and Simeon copyright © 1994, International Committee on English in the Liturgy, Inc.

This book was written by Peter Mazar and illustrated by Gertrud Mueller Nelson. It was edited by David Philippart with assistance from Pedro A. Vélez and Theresa Houston. It was designed by Anna Manhart and typeset in Galliard by Karen Mitchell. *Keeping Advent and Christmastime* was printed in the United States of America by Printing Arts Chicago.

Keeping Advent and Christmastime © 1996, Archdiocese of Chicago: Liturgy Training Publications, 1800 North Hermitage Avenue, Chicago IL 60622-1101; 1-800-933-1800; orders@ltp.org; fax 1-800-933-7094. All rights reserved. Visit our website at www.ltp.org.

Library of Congress Catalog Card Number 96-77206

ISBN 1-56854-027-2
KAC3

04 03 02 01   6 5 4 3

CONTENTS

INTRODUCTION

We Christians hold a great festival during the winter solstice, the shortest days of the year. We call this festival "Christmas," meaning the "feast of Christ." It takes several weeks to *prepare* and several weeks to *celebrate*.

The weeks of *preparation* are called Advent — the season of growing darkness before the solstice. The weeks of *celebration* are called Christmastime — the season of growing light after the solstice. Perhaps it comes down to something basic: We are children of light.

Of course, there's a great contrast between these two seasons of our faith and the commercial "holiday season." The "holiday season" begins in November and then comes to a crashing halt on December 25. But we Christians own Advent and Christmastime. The symbols of these seasons are our property, not advertisers' gimmicks. So it's important that we keep Advent and Christmas in church and at home according to our tradition.

And they're worth keeping. We *need* Advent. Without it we stop being what we are: a people who are waiting. We need the gospel's terrifying announcement of the end of time. We need the prophet's consolations and threats. We learn who we are in the uneasy raving of John the Baptist and in the gentle strength of Holy Mary.

And we need Christmastime. We need a festival that runs beyond a single day, beyond a single week. We need time to tell about the journey of the Magi, about the embrace of old Simeon and Anna, about the babbling of water made wine and the leaping Jordan and that glorious voice thundering what we yearn to hear: You are my beloved child!

In the days of Christmastime we shout loud and clear that Jesus Christ is born. The reign of God is here among us, in our own flesh and blood. That's why we gather around the star-topped tree of life and tinsel our homes in silver and gold, and spread our tables with the bounty of the harvest. The marvels of Christmas are signs of God's reign, signs of a life that conquers death, of "the light shining on in darkness, a darkness that did not overcome it" *(John 1:5)*.

Of course, Advent cannot exist if we jump the gun on Christmas. And Christmastime cannot exist if we are already tired of it by December 25. These two seasons require each other. Only after the silence of Advent can the carols of Christmastime spring. Only after Advent's darkness can a single star give so much cheer. Only after Advent's terror can an angel be heard, once again, telling us to "fear not." Year after year, we so genuinely need these seasons as rehearsal for heaven.

This festival of the winter solstice — this "feast of Christ" — does more than lead us from one year to another. In the power of Christ, Advent and Christmastime lead us from time into eternity.

ADVENT

Advent arrives gradually, like leaves falling off a tree until its summer glory becomes, in the words of Shakespeare, "bare ruin'd choirs where late the sweet birds sang." This image is found in the words of Isaiah and repeated in our prayers: "We have all withered like leaves, and our guilt carries us, away like the wind" *(Isaiah 64:5)*.

The despoiling of the world, the frosting of gardens, the slow ebbing of daylight: These are all warnings, as sharp as the prophets, as loud as John the Baptist, badgering us to face injustice, suffering, war — and the labor required of us to prepare the royal highway for the Sun of Justice, the Healer and the Comforter, the Prince of Peace.

At the same time, Advent arrives suddenly, without warning, a startling change "in the twinkling of an eye,"

like a snowfall that transforms the landscape. This image is proclaimed keenly in the gospel warnings of the end of time, a terror made more terrifying by the darkening of the sun and the waning of the moon. With Jeremiah we wail: "The harvest is past, the summer is ended, and yet we are not saved" *(Jeremiah 8:20)*.

Advent is the church's winter, with its darkness, its cold, the threat of starvation, the threat of death. And here is the paradox: In such a fearful night, the lighting of candles brings great joy. In such a numbing silence, the Spirit and the bride sing, "Come." It is the wondrous paradox of God's reign, where the desert blooms, the mountains are made low, where swords are beaten into plowshares and a virgin is found to be with child. Maranatha! Come, Lord Jesus! *(Revelation 22:20)*.

Blessing of the Advent Wreath

An evergreen wreath suspended from the ceiling, slowly turning while candles flicker in its branches, calls to mind a royal crown, or a victory wreath or even the wheel of time itself. An Advent wreath is a show of confidence that Christ is crowned the victor over evil. Christ will reach down through time to lead us into eternal light.

An Advent wreath is made with four candles arising from a circle of branches. It can be placed on a table or it can be hung over it with wide ribbons. Traditionally the wreath is hung where the Christmas tree will stand. The evergreen wreath is a foretaste of the evergreen tree. The four candles of Advent blossom into the countless lights of Christmastime.

A single candle is lit every evening during the week that begins with the Saturday before the first Sunday of Advent. Two candles are lit during the second week, three during the third and all four during the final week.

Candle lighting begins Advent evening prayer. Before the first candle is lit, the wreath may be blessed with this prayer:

By day and by night,
and through every season,
you watch over us, Lord.

We praise you for this Advent wreath.
It is the evergreen crown
   of your royal people,
and it shines with the promise
   of eternal victory.

By the light of this wreath
we shall wait in patience
   for your Son,
our Lord Jesus Christ,
who comforts our fears
and brings hope to the world.

All glory be yours
   now and for ever. Amen.

Then the first candle is lit and Advent evening prayer begins. See page 18.

Special Days

Saint Nicholas, *December 6*

(Jeremiah 1:4–10)

Without warning, Bishop Nicholas enters. It is a foretaste of Judgment Day! Nicholas exposes all the petty injustices of the home: who lies, who cheats, who is loud and who is lazy. Then in the triumph of mercy, he grants pardon in the form of tangerines and candy canes but not without a coal-black threat to the worst among us. Even if he is the patron of children, a visit from St. Nicholas is not child's play!

The Immaculate Conception, *December 8*

Our Lady of Guadalupe, *December 12*

(Zechariah 2:14–17)

We remember Mary's conception in her mother's womb. And we remember her appearance as a native Mexican, expectant with child, shining like the sun and moon together. In Advent Holy Mary teaches us how to wait. She is the wise virgin robed in midnight blue, patiently awaiting the groom *(Matthew 25:1–13)*. And she is the pregnant one, robed in the blood-red of the Spirit, yearning to see God cradled in her own arms *(Luke 1:26–38)*.

Saint Lucy, *December 13*

(MATTHEW 25:1–13)

Rubbing the sleep from our eyes, we are awakened to cheerful light. The early morning gloom flees as the martyr Lucy arrives wearing a crown of candles, a wise virgin bearing her lamp. Lucy—whose very name means "light"—heralds the dawn with gleaming saffron breads, as yellow as the sun and as spiralled as time itself. She comes like a bride, radiant in a veil of stars. Can the Daystar and the Bridegroom be far behind?

Hanukkah,

Begins six days before the new moon of December.

(1 MACCABEES 4:36–59)

We celebrate a miracle: A single day's worth of oil for the lamp of the Temple lasted eight days, a symbol of eternal light. Potato pancakes and round doughnuts fried in oil are customary treats during this season of the olive harvest—all circular signs of the sun! Although this eight-day festival commemorates brave warriors and great battles, the marvel that is most remembered is gentle light shining in the darkness.

The O Antiphons

The final week of Advent is like the stillness of night just
before dawn, or the yearning of bride and bridegroom
as the wedding day draws near, or the expectancy of
a mother as the child kicks in her womb. During this final
week we mark each day by singing an O Antiphon, one
each day, perhaps in our prayer at night. These antiphons
are familiar to us in the song "O come, O come,
Emmanuel."

December 17

O come, O Wisdom from on high,
Who governs all things tenderly;
To us the path of knowledge show,
And teach us in her ways to go. R.

December 18

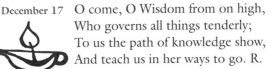

O come, O come, great Lord of might,
Who to your tribes on Sinai's height
In ancient times once gave the law
In cloud and majesty and awe. R.

December 19

O come, O Flower of Jesse's Root,
Before whom all the world stands mute.
We trust your mighty pow'r to save
And give us vict'ry o'er the grave. R.

December 20

O come, O Key of David, come
And open wide our heav'nly home.
Make safe the way that leads on high,
And close the path to misery. R.

December 21

O come, O Dayspring, come with cheer;
O Sun of Justice, now draw near.
Disperse the gloomy clouds of night,
And death's dark shadow put to flight. R.

December 22

O come, O Keystone, come and bind
In one the hearts of humankind.
Come bid our sad divisions cease,
And be for us the King of peace. R.

December 23

O come, O come, Emmanuel,
And ransom captive Israel
That mourns in lonely exile here
Until the Son of God appear. R.

Refrain: Rejoice, rejoice,
Emmanuel shall come to you,
O Israel.

MORNING PRAYER

John the Baptist, our Advent watchman, announces the dawn. The rising sun brings with it the promise of the coming of Christ, the Sun of Justice, who will rise over us "with healing in his wings" *(Malachi 3:20)*.

Sign of the Cross

It is customary to sign ourselves with water as a morning remembrance of baptism.

In the name of the Father
    and of the Son
    and of the Holy Spirit.

It is now the hour for us to wake from sleep.
The night is far spent; the day draws near.
Let us cast off deeds of darkness
    and put on the armor of light.

ROMANS 13:11–12

Hymn

The following song may be sung, either to its own beautiful melody or to any common meter tune, such as "O God, our help in ages past."

The King shall come when morning dawns
    And light triumphant breaks,
when beauty gilds the eastern hills
    And life to joy awakes.

Not as, of old, a little child
    To suffer and to die,
But crowned with glory like the sun
    That lights the morning sky.

The King shall come when morning dawns
    And light and beauty brings.
Hail, Christ the Lord! your people pray:
    Come quickly, King of kings!

Psalm 85

I listen to God speaking:
"I, the Lord, speak peace,
peace to my faithful people
who turn their hearts to me."
Salvation is coming near,
glory is filling our land.

Love and fidelity embrace,
peace and justice kiss.
Fidelity sprouts from the earth,
justice leans down from heaven.

The Lord pours out riches,
our land springs to life.
Justice clears God's path,
justice points the way.

PSALM 85:9 – 14

Daily Scripture

The daily scripture may be read now, or at evening prayer.
See the chart on pages 22 – 23.

The Song of Zechariah

Praise the Lord, the God of Israel,
who shepherds the people and sets them free.

God raises from David's house
a child with power to save.

Through the holy prophets
God promised in ages past
to save us from enemy hands,
from the grip of all who hate us.

The Lord favored our ancestors
recalling the sacred covenant,
the pledge to our ancestor Abraham,
to free us from our enemies,
so we might worship without fear
and be holy and just all our days.

And you, child, will be called
Prophet of the Most High,
for you will come to prepare
a pathway for the Lord
by teaching the people salvation
through forgiveness of their sin.

Out of God's deepest mercy
a dawn will come from on high,
light for those shadowed by death,
a guide for our feet on the way to peace.

Lord's Prayer

*Morning prayer concludes with the Our Father. A sign of peace
may be exchanged.*

Evening Prayer

The lamps we kindle every evening were given to us
at baptism to keep burning brightly through the night.
On these Advent evenings, when darkness descends
so early, we trim our lamps like the wise virgin, eagerly
awaiting the coming of the Lord, our beloved
bridegroom (see *Matthew 25:1–13*).

Candle Lighting

A candle or the Advent wreath is lit:

Blessed are you, Lord, God of all creation!
You bring forth light from darkness.

After the candle is lit:

I form the light and create the darkness.
I make well-being and create woe.
I, the Lord do all these things!

or:

Let justice descend, O heavens, like dew from above.
Like gentle rain let the skies drop it down.
Let the earth open and salvation bud forth.

Isaiah 45:7–8

Hymn

This ancient hymn may be sung to its own beautiful melody or any long meter tune, such as "Praise God from whom all blessings flow."

O Savior, rend the heavens wide!
  Come down, come down with mighty stride.
Unlock the gates, the doors break down;
  Unbar the way to heaven's crown.

O earth, in flow'ring bud be seen,
  Clothe hill and dale in garb of green.
Drop down, you clouds, the life of spring.
  From Jacob's line rain down the King.

Come, Child of God! Without your light
  We grope in dread and gloom of night.
  Come lead us with a gentle hand
  From exile to the promised land.

Psalm 25

Lord, I give myself to you.

Teach me how to live,
Lord, show me the way.
Steer me toward your truth,
you, my saving God,
you, my constant hope.

Recall your tenderness,
your lasting love.
Remember me, not my faults,
the sins of my youth.
To show your own goodness,
God, remember me.

Protect me and save my life.
Keep me from disgrace,
for I take shelter in you.
Let integrity stand guard
as I wait for you.

Free Israel, O God,
from all its troubles.

PSALM 25:1, 4–7, 20–22

Daily Scripture

The daily scripture may be read after dinner. See the chart on pages 22–23.

The Song of Mary

I acclaim the greatness of the Lord,
I delight in God my savior,
who regarded my humble state.
Truly from this day on
all ages will call me blest.

For God, wonderful in power,
has used that strength for me.
Holy the name of the Lord!
whose mercy embraces the faithful,
one generation to the next.

The mighty arm of God
scatters the proud in their conceit,
pulls tyrants from their thrones,
and raises up the humble.
The Lord fills the starving
and lets the rich go hungry.

God rescues lowly Israel,
recalling the promise of mercy,
the promise made to our ancestors,
to Abraham's heirs for ever.

Intercessions and the Lord's Prayer

At day's end we offer our petitions to the Father in Jesus' name.
We seal these prayers with the Our Father and a sign of peace.

Scriptures

First Sunday of Advent

(A) 2001, 2004	Isaiah 2:1–5	Romans 13:11–14	Matthew 24:37–44
(B) 2002, 2005	Is. 63:16—64:7	1 Corinthians 1:3–9	Mark 13:33–37
(C) 2003, 2006	Jer. 33:14–16	1 Thes. 3:12—4:2	Luke 21:25–28, 34–36

Weekdays

Monday	Isaiah 2:1–5	Matthew 8:5–11
Tuesday	Isaiah 11:1–10	Luke 10:21–24
Wednesday	Isaiah 25:6–10	Matthew 15:29–37
Thursday	Isaiah 26:1–6	Matthew 7:21–27
Friday	Isaiah 29:17–24	Matthew 9:27–31
Saturday	Isaiah 30:19–26	Matthew 9:35—10:8

Second Sunday of Advent

(A) 2001, 2004	Isaiah 11:1–10	Romans 15:4–9	Matthew 3:1–12
(B) 2002, 2005	Isaiah 40:1–11	2 Peter 3:8–14	Mark 1:1–8
(C) 2003, 2006	Baruch 5:1–9	Philippians 1:3–11	Luke 3:1–6

Weekdays

Monday	Isaiah 35:1–10	Luke 5:17–26
Tuesday	Isaiah 40:1–11	Matthew 18:12–14
Wednesday	Isaiah 40:25–31	Matthew 11:28–30
Thursday	Isaiah 41:13–20	Matthew 11:11–15
Friday	Isaiah 48:17–19	Matthew 11:16–19
Saturday	Sirach 48:1–11	Matthew 17:10–13

Third Sunday of Advent

(A) 2001, 2004	Isaiah 35:1–10	James 5:7–10	Matthew 11:1–11
(B) 2002 2005	Isaiah 61:1–11	1 Thes. 5:16–24	John 1:6–8, 19–28
(C) 2003, 2006	Zep. 3:14–18	Philippians 4:4–7	Luke 3:10–18

Weekdays up to December 16

	Monday	Numbers 24:1–19	Matthew 21:23–27
	Tuesday	Zephaniah 3:1–13	Matthew 21:28–32
	Wednesday	Isaiah 45:5–25	Luke 7:18–23
	Thursday	Isaiah 54:1–10	Luke 7:24–30
	Friday	Isaiah 56:1–8	John 5:33–36

Fourth Sunday of Advent

(A) 2001, 2004	Isaiah 7:10–14	Romans 1:1–7	Matthew 1:18–24
(B) 2002, 2005	2 Samuel 7:1–16	Romans 16:25–27	Luke 1:26–38
(C) 2003, 2006	Micah 5:1–4	Hebrews 10:5–10	Luke 1:39–45

Weekdays after December 16

	December 17	Genesis 49:1–27	Matthew 1:1–17
	December 18	Jeremiah 23:1–8	Matthew 1:18–24
	December 19	Judges 13:2–25	Luke 1:5–25
	December 20	Isaiah 7:10–14	Luke 1:26–38
	December 21	Song of Songs 2:1–17	Luke 1:39–45
	December 22	1 Samuel 1:1—2:11	Luke 1:46–56
	December 23	Malachi 3:1–24	Luke 1:57–66
	December 24	2 Samuel 7:1–16	Luke 1:67–79

ADVENT AND CHRISTMASTIME NIGHT PRAYER

Night is a time of watchfulness and a time of sleep. It can bring the greatest anxiety or the greatest contentment. Our final prayer of the day can be made at bedside, perhaps said kneeling during Advent and standing during Christmastime.

May almighty God give us a restful night
　and a peaceful death.

Hymn

A verse of any carol may be sung, such as "O come, O come, Emmanuel" during Advent, or "Silent Night" during Christmastime, or this beautiful carol appropriate during both seasons.

Lo, how a Rose e'er blooming
　From tender stem has sprung!
Of Jesse's lineage coming
　As seers of old have sung.
It comes, a blossom bright,
　Amid the cold of winter,
When half spent is the night.

Psalm 131

Lord, I am not proud,
holding my head too high,
reaching beyond my grasp.

No, I am calm and tranquil
like a weaned child
resting in its mother's arms:
my whole being at rest.

Let Israel rest in the Lord,
now and for ever.

Song of Simeon

Lord, let your servant
now die in peace,
for you kept your promise.

With my own eyes
I see the salvation
you prepared for all peoples:

a light of revelation for the Gentiles
and glory to your people Israel.

The Sign of the Cross

We end the day as we began, with the sign of the cross:

May the almighty and merciful Lord,
   the Father and Son and the Holy Spirit,
   bless and keep us. Amen.

Invocation to Mary

*The final prayer of the day is traditionally to Mother Mary,
such as the "Hail, Mary." Here is a prayer for Advent and
Christmastime,* Alma Redemptoris Mater:

O loving mother of our Savior,
   forever-abiding gate of heaven
   and star of the sea,
O hasten to aid us, who oft falling,
   strive to rise again.

Maiden, while nature stood in awe,
   you gave birth to your own maker,
   to your all-holy Lord.
Virgin ever, after as before,
   through the mouth of Gabriel
   heaven spoke its *Ave:*
Have compassion on us sinners!

CHRISTMAS EVE

Christmas Eve is a night of wonder. We stand between the expectancy of Advent and the jubilation of Christmas.

The day before Christmas is traditionally a fast day in preparation for the feast to come. The evening meal breaks the fast with simple tokens of the harvest — fruits, nuts, seeds and salad — all signs of the harvest of God's reign. Meat is not eaten for the animals themselves were first to behold their Lord, lying in their own manger. Many nationalities eat seafood — a reminder that the messiah will slaughter the scaly seabeast Leviathan, death itself (see *Psalm 74* and *Isaiah 27*), and invite everyone to a heavenly fish-fry (see *John 21*).

An empty place may be set for the dead or the distant, or for any stranger. Straw may be spread under the tablecloth or under the table itself. Many households begin the meal by breaking a festive bread, dipping the pieces in honey and sharing them with wishes for a sweet Christmas. In this way we make our homes a new Bethlehem, a word that means "the house of bread."

Three simple ceremonies for Christmas Eve are the lighting of Christmas lights, the lighting and blessing of the tree, and the blessing of the crèche, the manger scene. Of course, these ceremonies have great power if Christmas Eve is the first night you light the tree and lights — a great burst of light to welcome Christ!

On Christmas Eve the household can gather for Christmastime evening prayer *(page 42)*.

Blessing of the Christmas Tree

The lighting of the Christmas tree on Christmas Eve can be part of evening prayer, page 42. The first time the tree is lit, it may be blessed with this prayer. The household gathers around the tree as one person prays:

God of Adam and Eve,
    God of all our ancestors,
    we praise you for this tree.
It stirs a memory of paradise
and brings a foretaste of heaven.

Send your Son,
    the flower of the root of Jesse,
to restore your good earth
to the freshness of creation.

Then every tree of the forest
    will clap its hands,
and all creation will bless you
    from these shining branches.

All glory be yours
now and for ever. Amen.

The tree is now lit and evening prayer may begin. See page 42.

Blessing of the Crèche

This blessing can end evening prayer (page 42) on Christmas Eve or begin morning prayer (page 38) on Christmas Day. The household gathers near the manger scene. Candles may be lit and flowers placed nearby. Someone prays the blessing:

Bless us, Lord,
   as we come to Bethlehem
where animals and angels,
   shepherds and seekers
together behold your face.

Here snow becomes straw
   and frost becomes flowers
as winter melts into everlasting spring.

In our holy Christmas
   give us the riches of your poverty.
Show us the wonder of simplicity
as we join the angels
   in proclaiming your praise:
Glory in heaven and peace on earth,
   now and for ever. Amen.

The figure of the Christ child is now placed in the manger, and all sing "Joy to the World," "Silent Night" or any favorite carol.

CHRISTMASTIME

No sooner does the winter sun turn in its course back toward the summertime than we Christians latch onto this tiny sign of hope and make midwinter our second spring. Christmas is a festival of birth, and birth is, after all, a springtime event. How harsh a contradiction to celebrate birth when winter is just beginning! Yet "new birth" is our cry: Noel!

So we banish the long nights with firelight and candles. We defy the winter by festooning summer's green from our rafters. We spread our tables with the abundance of the harvest, all signs of God's graciousness, signs of the bounty of heaven itself. We gather around the sparkling tree of life and declare this place, no matter how humble, to be paradise.

We celebrate a birth, not a birthday. Christmas is not Jesus' birthday. It is not an anniversary of something

that happened long ago. Christmas is a celebration of the birth of Christ, now, *hodie*, today.

This word "today" is a key to entering into the mystery of Christmastime, for if Christ is born today that means we can see and touch and hold Christ. It also means that we must feed and clothe and protect Christ, now, *hodie*, today.

One of the hallmarks of genuine Christian celebration is this combination of tremendous comfort and joys with tremendous challenge. No wonder it takes so many days to keep Christmastime! And no wonder we keep Christmastime by renewing our efforts to clothe the naked, to feed the hungry and to bring together neighbors and strangers alike to share in *Christes Messe*, the feast of Christ.

Hodie Christus natus est. Noel!

31

Special Days

Christmas Day, *December 25*

(John 1:1–17)

Christmas is for party games, the sillier the better. There's the piñata, a sign of heaven showering down graciousness. Or there's parcheesi, a retracing of the search of the Magi for the home of Christ. Or there's pin-the-tail-on-the-donkey, the kindly animal who carried the Holy Family to Egypt. Or snapdragons: whoever can pluck the most raisins scattered on a plate of flaming rum wins a kiss from everyone there.

Saint Stephen, *December 26*

(Acts 7:54 – 60)

Today is called "Boxing Day" because it's customary to bring "Stephen's boxes" of food to the poor like Deacon Stephen did. It's a fine day to mail a check to charity. Who could use a boxful — or an earful — of Christmas cheer? Good King Wenceslaus knows! Christmastime is for caroling, bringing folks door-to-door hospitality as we remember that "ye who now shall bless the poor, shall yourselves find blessings."

Saint John, *December 27*

(1 John 1:1–5)

On John's feast day we toast the beloved disciple with these ancient words: "Wassail! I drink to you the love of Saint John!" Legend has it that John drank poisoned wine without harm. Another tradition is that John outlived all the other disciples. He obviously had plenty of wassail—which means "good health." The Lord Jesus comes to make us hale and hearty "with healing in his wings" *(Malachi 3:20)*.

The Holy Innocents, *December 28*

(Matthew 2:13–23)

Today death is placed side by side with birth. And why such a day of sorrow within these days of Christmas? Perhaps if told at any other season this story of such cruelty might make our faith seem absurd. Throughout every generation there are Herods who begrudge each new generation its very existence. Today we remember all holy innocents of every time and place. For Rachel has not ceased her weeping.

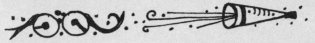

New Year's Eve, *December 31*

(ECCLESIASTES 3:1–15)

Go a bit crazy tonight. Act like it's Doom's Day. Be crazy enough to open your door to your neighbors, to ask pardon of those you've hurt, to extend affection to everyone you meet. The custom of making a racket at midnight is simply an act of kindness. No one should be caught asleep when the master returns (see *Luke 12:35–40*). Take the camaraderie of Christmas to the streets with bells and horns and hugs and kisses.

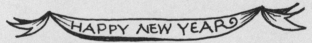

New Year's Day, *January 1*

(LUKE 2:16–21)

New Year's midnight is the halfway mark in the Twelve Days of Christmas—the jolly days in which we honor Christ as the Lord of past, present and future. Today is a customary occasion to bless all the members of your household, a day for hospitality, as if the whole world is having open house! Spend some time reminiscing and telling stories of births and beginnings, like Holy Mary, "treasuring all these things in her heart."

Epiphany, *January 6* *

(MATTHEW 2:1–12)

The word "epiphany" means "showing forth." Epiphany
is a triple celebration of the adoration of the Magi, the
baptism of Jesus in the Jordan and the wedding feast of
Cana. Stars and clouds, gold and incense, wine and
water, rivers and skies, every element in the universe
shows forth the good news: Jesus Christ is Lord! Today
is the fulfillment of Advent, the merriest day of our
merry Christmastime. * *Epiphany is kept on the Sunday
after New Year's in Canada and the U.S.A.*

Baptism of the Lord, *the Sunday after Epiphany* *

(PSALM 29)

If on Christmas Day we rejoiced to see Jesus with
his mother, today we rejoice to see Jesus with his father.
From the heavens a proud papa thunders his affection.
The name "Jesus" is a variation of "Joshua" — meaning
"Savior." The Lord Jesus is our new Joshua who leads
us through the Jordan of baptism into the land of milk
and honey. Surely an eggnog toast is in order on this
final day of Christmastime! * *In years when Epiphany is
kept on January 7 or 8, the Baptism of the Lord is kept on the
Monday after Epiphany.*

Epiphany Blessing of the Home

Epiphany is the traditional day for this blessing — but any day you can gather the household during Christmastime is a good day for it.

Divide a mince pie — or any cake — into as many pieces as you have participants. Hide a coin or dry bean in one piece and distribute at random. Whoever gets the coin or bean is crowned (party hat?), robed (comics taped together?), saluted (noisemakers?) and toasted (hot, buttered what-have-you) as king or queen of the new year.

The newly crowned royalty now writes the following with chalk over the front door of the home:

$$20 + C + M + B + 01$$

The numerals are those of the new year. The four crosses are the four seasons. *C-M-B* are the initials of the legendary names of the Magi — Caspar, Melchior and Balthasar.

The blessing of the home on the next page is then prayed. Now everyone moves from room to room sprinkling the home with water, a sign of Jesus' baptism in the River Jordan. Try singing a carol such as "We three kings" during this procession. When the sprinkling is complete, the Lord's Prayer is said by all, and then the greeting of peace is exchanged.

That's how we celebrate our God who makes
commoners and kings and queens. That's how we
welcome all strangers through our doors. For the star of
Epiphany shines over us, we who have passed through
the Jordan of baptism, we who bear the name of Christ.

*This blessing may be simple — said at mealtime and perhaps
followed by a sprinkling of the rooms of the home with water.
Or the blessing may be elaborate — part of the ritual described
on the previous page. This blessing may also be kept as the
conclusion to Christmastime evening prayer on page 42.*

God of all time and space,
with Christmas joy we praise you
    for the year gone by
and for the year we have begun.

May this home we have made
be filled with kindness to one another,
with hospitality to guests ·
and with abundant care for every stranger.

By the gentle light of a star
guide home all who seek you
on paths of wonder, peace and charity.

Fill the year with good gifts for all the world
as we join with the angels
    in proclaiming your praise:
Glory in heaven and peace on earth,
now and for ever. Amen.

Morning Prayer

Morning is a time of epiphany — of revelation. What is hidden in darkness is now bathed in light. On these merry Christmastime mornings we praise Christ, who is revealed in the waters of the Jordan as God's own beloved child, who is revealed in the heavens as the Morning Star that never sets.

The Sign of the Cross

It is customary to sign ourselves with water as a morning remembrance of baptism.

In the name of the Father
  and of the Son
  and of the Holy Spirit.

God's holy day has dawned for us at last.
Come, all you people, and adore the Lord!

Hymn

Christmastime is a singing season. A hymn or carol may be part of morning prayer.

O come, all ye faithful, joyful and triumphant,
  O come ye, O come ye to Bethlehem,
Come and behold him, born the King of angels.
O come, let us adore him, O come, let us adore him,
O come, let us adore him, Christ the Lord.

Yea, Lord we greet thee, born this happy morning.
   Jesus to thee be all glory given.
Word of the Father, now in flesh appearing!
O come, let us adore him, O come, let us adore him,
O come, let us adore him, Christ the Lord.

Psalm 72

God, give your king judgment,
the son of the king
your sense of what is right;
help him judge your people
and do right for the powerless.

May mountains bear peace,
hills bring forth justice.
May the king defend the poor,
set their children free,
and kill their oppressors.

May he live as long as the sun,
as long as the moon, for ever.
May he be like rain on a field,
like showers that soak the earth.

May justice sprout in his time,
peace till the moon is no more.
May he rule from sea to sea,
from the river to the ends of the earth.

Kings from Tarshish and the islands
will bring their riches to him.

Kings of Sheba, kings of Saba
will carry gifts to him.
All kings will bow before him,
all the nations serve him.

He will rescue the poor at their call,
those no one speaks for.
Those no one cares for
he hears and will save,
save their lives from violence,
lives precious in his eyes.

PSALM 72: 1–8, 10–14

Daily Scripture

The daily scripture may be read now or at evening prayer. See the chart on pages 46–47.

The Song of Zechariah

Praise the Lord, the God of Israel,
who shepherds the people and sets them free.

God raises from David's house
a child with power to save.
Through the holy prophets

God promised in ages past
to save us from enemy hands,
from the grip of all who hate us.

The Lord favored our ancestors
recalling the sacred covenant,
the pledge to our ancestor Abraham,
to free us from our enemies,
so we might worship without fear
and be holy and just all our days.

And you, child, will be called
Prophet of the Most High,
for you will come to prepare
a pathway for the Lord
by teaching the people salvation
through forgiveness of their sin.

Out of God's deepest mercy
a dawn will come from on high,
light for those shadowed by death,
a guide for our feet on the way to peace.

Lord's Prayer

*Morning prayer concludes with the Our Father. A sign of peace
may be exchanged.*

Evening Prayer

Every evening Christians kindle lamps to welcome
Christ, the light of the world. Christmastime is a season
for lighting lamps — the shining tree, candles in our
windows, strings of lights around our front doors. In
power and in glory, the coming of Christ drives the dark
winter away.

Candle Lighting

A candle or the Christmas tree is lit:

Blessed are you, Lord, God of all creation!
You bring forth light from darkness.

After the candle or tree is lit:

Rise up in splendor, Jerusalem!
Your light has come.
The glory of the Lord shines upon you.

or:

See, darkness covers the earth,
    and thick clouds cover the peoples;
But upon you the Lord shines
    and over you appears the Lord's glory.

Isaiah 60:1–2

Hymn

Christmastime is a singing season. A hymn or carol may be part of evening prayer.

Hark, the herald angels sing,
  "Glory to the newborn King!
Peace on earth and mercy mild,
  God and sinners reconciled!"
Joyful, all ye nations rise;
  Join the triumph of the skies;
With angelic hosts proclaim,
  "Christ is born in Bethlehem!"
Hark, the herald angels sing,
  "Glory to the newborn King!"

Hail the heav'n-born Prince of Peace!
  Hail the Sun of Righteousness!
Light and life to all he brings,
  Ris'n with healing in his wings.
Mild he lays his glory by,
  Born that we no more may die,
Born to raise us from the earth,
  Born to give us second birth.
Hark, the herald angels sing,
  "Glory to the newborn King!"

Psalm 98

Sing to the Lord a new song,
the Lord of wonderful deeds.

Shout to the Lord, you earth,
break into song, into praise!

Let roar the sea with its creatures,
the world and all that live there!
Let rivers clap their hands,
the hills ring out their joy!

The Lord our God comes,
comes to rule the earth,
justly to rule the world,
to govern the peoples aright.

PSALM 98:1A, 4, 7–9

Daily Scripture

The daily scripture may be read after dinner. See the chart on pages 46 – 47.

The Song of Mary

I acclaim the greatness of the Lord,
I delight in God my savior,
who regarded my humble state.

Truly from this day on
all ages will call me blest.

For God, wonderful in power,
has used that strength for me.
Holy the name of the Lord!
whose mercy embraces the faithful,
one generation to the next.

The mighty arm of God
scatters the proud in their conceit,
pulls tyrants from their thrones,
and raises up the humble.
The Lord fills the starving
and lets the rich go hungry.

God rescues lowly Israel,
recalling the promise of mercy,
the promise made to our ancestors,
to Abraham's heirs for ever.

Intercessions and Lord's Prayer

*At day's end we offer our petitions to the Father in Jesus' name.
During Christmastime we pray especially for those who cannot
share such a festival, the homeless and the abandoned, the lonely
and the grieving, as well as all the holy innocents of every time
and place.*

*We seal all these prayers with the Our Father. A sign of peace
may be exchanged.*

Scriptures

Christmas Day, December 25

Vigil	Isaiah 62:1–5	Acts 13:16–25	Matthew 1:1–25
Midnight	Isaiah 9:1–6	Titus 2:11–14	Luke 2:1–14
Dawn	Isaiah 62:11–12	Titus 3:4–7	Luke 2:15–20
Day	Isaiah 52:7–10	Hebrews 1:1–6	John 1:1–18

The Holy Family, the Sunday after Christmas Day *

(A) 2001, 2004	Sirach 3:1–16	Colossians 3:12–21	Mt. 2:13–15, 19–23
(B) 2002, 2005	Sirach 3:1–16	Colossians 3:12–21	Luke 2:22–40
(C) 2003, 2006	Sirach 3:1–16	Colossians 3:12–21	Luke 2:41–52

Weekdays between Christmas Day and New Year's

St. Stephen, December 26	Acts 6:8–10; 7:54–59	Matthew 10:17–22
St. John, December 27	1 John 1:1–4	John 20:2–8
Holy Innocents, December 28	1 John 1:5—2:2	Matthew 2:13–18
December 29	1 John 2:3–11	Luke 2:22–35
December 30	1 John 2:12–17	Luke 2:36–40
December 31	1 John 2:18–21	John 1:1–18

Mary, the Mother of God, January 1

(A, B, C)	Nm. 6:22–27	Galatians 4:4–7	Luke 2:16–21

Weekdays between New Year's Day and Epiphany

January 2	1 John 2:22–28	John 1:19–28
January 3	1 John 2:29—3:6	John 1:29–34
January 4	1 John 3:7–10	John 1:35–42
January 5	1 John 3:11–21	John 1:43–51
January 6	1 John 5:5–13	Matthew 1:7–11
January 7	1 John 5:14–21	John 2:1–12

The Epiphany of the Lord, January 6 **

(A, B, C)   Isaiah 60:1–6   Eph. 3:2–3, 5–6   Matthew 2:1–12

Weekdays between Epiphany and Baptism of the Lord

Monday	1 John 3:22—4:6	Matthew 4:12–17, 23–25
Tuesday	1 John 4:7–10	Mark 6:34–44
Wednesday	1 John 4:11–18	Mark 6:45–52
Thursday	1 John 4:19—5:4	Luke 4:14–22
Friday	1 John 5:5–13	Luke 5:12–16
Saturday	1 John 5:14–21	John 3:22–30

The Baptism of the Lord, the Sunday after Epiphany **

A) 2002, 2005	Isaiah 42:1–7	Acts 10:34–38	Matthew 3:13–17
B) 2003, 2006	Isaiah 42:1–7	Acts 10:34–38	Mark 1:7–11
C) 2004, 2007	Isaiah 42:1–7	Acts 10:34–38	Luke 3:15–22

* *If the Sunday after Christmas Day is January 1, the Feast of the Holy Family is celebrated on December 30.*
** *In the United States and Canada, the Epiphany of the Lord is celebrated on the Sunday after January 1. The Baptism of the Lord is celebrated on the Sunday after Epiphany, unless Epiphany is kept on January 7 or 8, in which case the Baptism of the Lord is observed on the Monday after Epiphany.*

CANDLEMAS

By Candlemas, February 2, the Feast of the Presentation of the Lord in the Temple, the worst of winter is past. Day is lengthening rapidly. The "lengthen season" — the meaning of the word "Lent" — comes soon. The world aches for springtime.

On Christmas Day a light was kindled. On Epiphany this light rose to twinkle from the stars. And today this starlight is placed in our very arms. We are hand-in-hand with God.

Today the Christmas crèche is surrounded with candles and with the very first of spring flowers, even if these have to be brought inside and coaxed into early bloom. Then the crèche is dismantled. Like old Simeon and Anna, Christmas departs in peace.

Lent is coming! The light in our arms must be sacrificed. We must be ready to lose our lives. We must ache for Easter.